# The Ultimate Beginner Series
# Acoustic Guitar Basics
## Steps One & Two Combined

Alfred Publishing Co., Inc.
16320 Roscoe Blvd., Suite 100
P.O. Box 10003
Van Nuys, CA 91410-0003
alfred.com

Copyright © MCMXCIV, MCMXCVI, MMVII by Alfred Publishing Co., Inc.
All rights reserved. Printed in USA.

ISBN-10: 1-57623-425-8 (Book & CD)
ISBN-13: 978-1-57623-425-9 (Book & CD)

Cover guitar courtesy Gibson Musical Instruments.

# *Section One: The Basics*

**CD**
**③** *The Three Basic Guitar Types*

**Nylon String Acoustic**
**(Classic Guitar)**

The nylon string acoustic guitar has a nice mellow tone and has several advantages for beginners. The strings are much easier to press to the fretboard so they don't cut into your fingers the way steel strings do. Also, the neck is wider than on a typical steel string guitar which makes fingering chords a little easier. The classic guitar is perfectly suited to intimate, unaccompanied guitar performances.

**The Electric Guitar**

The electric guitar has come to dominate popular music. It is an extremely versatile instrument capable of producing everything from mellow jazz tones and biting funk riffs to the screaming, over-the-top, dizzying pyro-technics of rock's reigning guitar virtuosos.

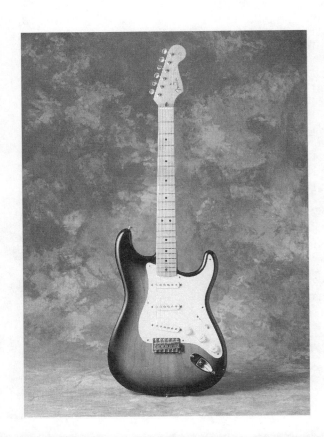

**The Steel String Acoustic**

The steel string acoustic guitar is perhaps the most versatile and common guitar type. Although it is a little bit harder to play than the nylon string guitar, the steel string acoustic has a loud, bright, ringing tone that clearly projects to the listener. The steel-string acoustic is the backbone of most country and bluegrass bands. It's perfect for backing a singer and, in the hands of today's new acoustic performers, its stylistic palette encompasses everything from New Age and Country Blues, to hot Bluegrass flatpicking, jazz fusion and "unplugged" rock.

## *Parts of the Guitar*

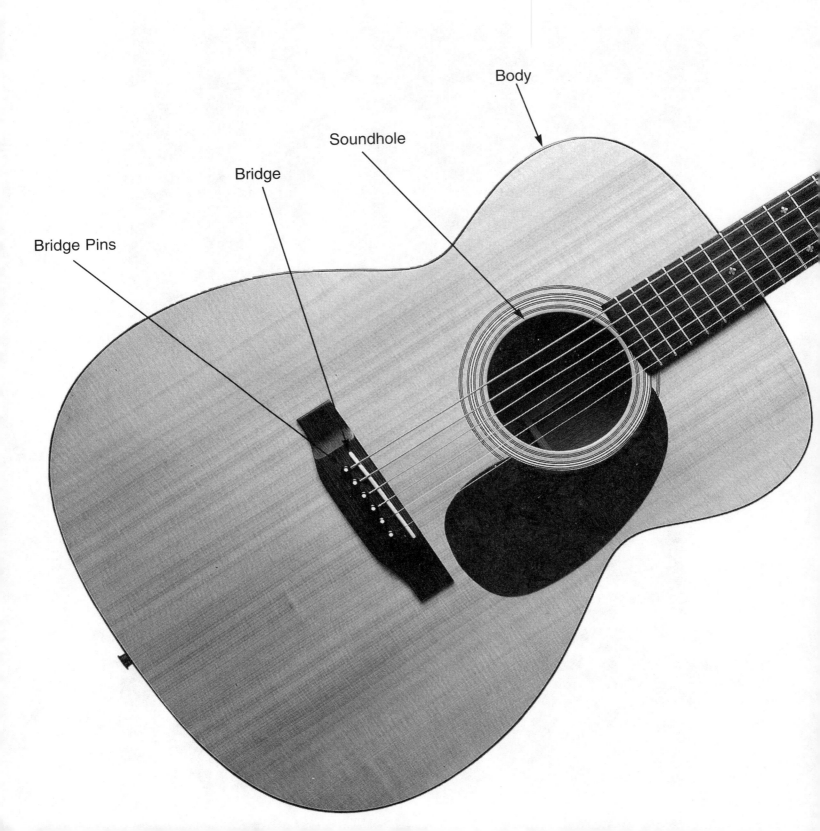

Body

Soundhole

Bridge

Bridge Pins

Tuning Pegs (string attached here)

Headstock

Fingerboard

Nut

Frets, 1st, 2nd, etc

Strings 1-6
(low to high in pitch)

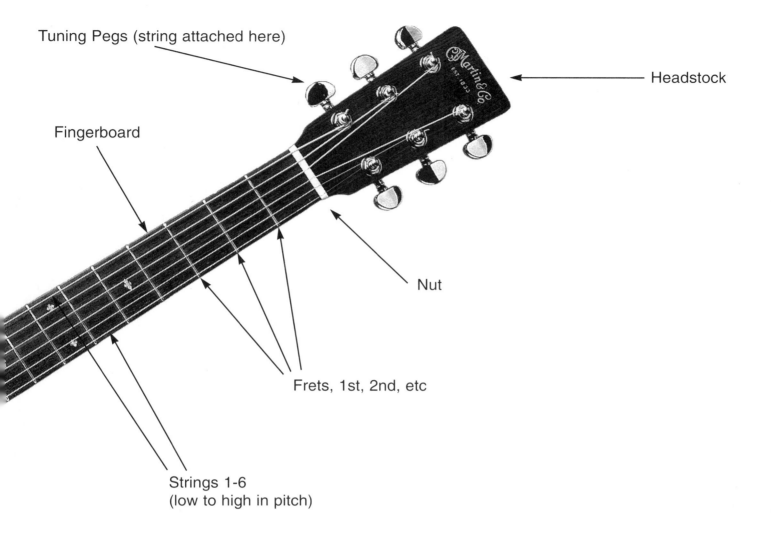

**Strings:** Strings are available in three basic gauges, light, medium and heavy. I suggest you begin with light or medium gauge strings.

**Picks:** Picks come in many shapes, sizes and thicknesses. For acoustic guitar, I recommend light to medium thickness. For electric, the thicker picks seem to work best. Experiment to find the size and shape you are most comfortable with.

**CD**
**(4) Tuning Methods**

## Tuning to a Keyboard:

The six strings of a guitar can be tuned to a keyboard by matching the sound of each open guitar string to the keyboard notes as indicated in the diagram.

Note: You will hear the intonation better, and your guitar will stay in better tune, if you loosen the strings and tune them **up** to pitch rather than bringing them from above the pitch and tuning down.

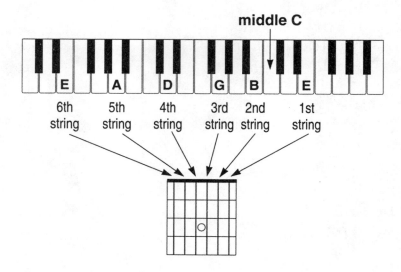

## Electronic Tuners:

Many brands of small, battery operated tuners are available. These are excellent for keeping your guitar in perfect tune and for developing your ear to hear intonation very accurately. Simply follow the instructions supplied with the electronic tuner.

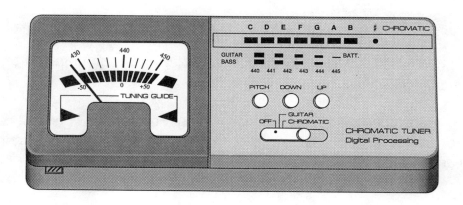

**Tuning the Guitar to Itself – The "Fifth Fret" Method:**

1) Either assume your 6th string "E" is in tune or tune it to a piano or some other fixed pitch instrument.

2) Depress the 6th string at the 5th fret. Play it and you will hear the note "A," which is the same as the 5th string played open. Turn the 5th string tuning key until the pitch of the open 5th string (A) matches that of the 6th string/5th fret (also A).

3) Depress the 5th string at the 5th fret. Play it and you will hear the note "D," which is the same as the 4th string played open. Turn the 4th string tuning key until the pitch of the open 4th string (D) matches that of the 5th string/5th fret (also D).

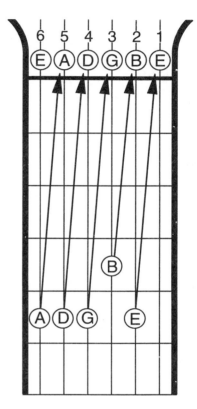

4) Depress the 4th string at the 5th fret. Play it and you will hear the note "G," which is the same as the 3rd string played open. Turn the 3rd string tuning key until the pitch of the open 3rd string (G) matches that of the 4th string/5th fret (also G).

5) Depress the 3rd string at the 4th fret (not the 5th fret as in the other strings). Play it and you will hear the note "B," which is the same as the 2nd string played open. Turn the 2nd string tuning key until the pitch of the open 2nd string (B) matches that of the 3rd string/4th fret (also B).

6) Depress the 2nd string at the 5th fret. Play it and you will hear the note "E," which is the same as the 1st string played open. Turn the 1st string tuning key until the pitch of the open 1st string (E) matches that of the 2nd string/5th fret (also E).

## Changing Strings

Eventually, whether because a string has broken on its own, or because through repeated use it is no longer "tunable," you will have to change your strings. Be prepared! Always keep in your guitar case:

1) A set of extra strings

2) A pair of wire cutters          All available at your local music store.

3) A string winder

**Changing Strings:**

1) First, remove the bridge pin to release the ball end from the bridge. Unwrap the other end of the string from around the tuning peg.

2) Insert the ball end of the new string into the hole in the bridge and replace the bridge pin.

3) Once the string has been inserted into the bridge, feed the other end through the hole in the tuning peg, make sure to leave some slack in the string.

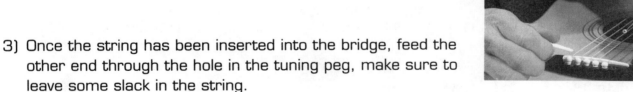

4) Bend the end slightly, and with your string winder, begin to tighten the string.

5) Trim the excess string off with your wire cutters.

## *Reading Rhythm Notation*

At the beginning of every song is a time signature. 4/4 is the most common time signature:

**4**      FOUR COUNTS TO A MEASURE
**4**      A QUARTER NOTE RECEIVES ONE COUNT

The top number tells you how many counts per measure.
The bottom number tells you which kind of note receives one count.

The time value of a note is determined by three things:

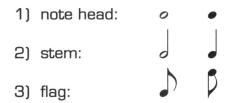

1) note head:

2) stem:

3) flag:

**o**  This is a whole note. The note head is open and has no stem. In 4/4 time a whole note receives 4 counts.

This is a half note. It has an open note head and a stem. A half note receives 2 counts.

This is a quarter note. It has a solid note head and a stem. A quarter note receives 1 count.

This is an eighth note. It has a solid note head and a stem with a flag attached. An eighth note receives 1/2 count.

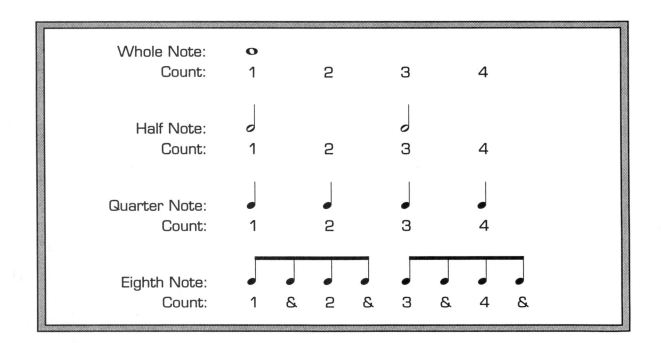

## *Reading Music Notation*

Music is written on a **staff**. The staff consists of five lines and four spaces between the lines:

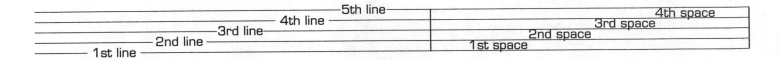

The names of the notes are the same as the first seven letters of the alphabet: A B C D E F G.

The notes are written in alphabetical order. The first (lowest) line is "E":

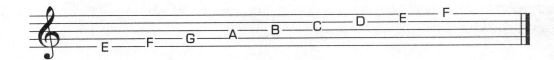

Notes can extend above and below the staff. When they do, **ledger lines** are added. Here is the approximate range of the guitar from the lowest note, open 6th string "E," to a "B" on the 1st string at the 17th fret.

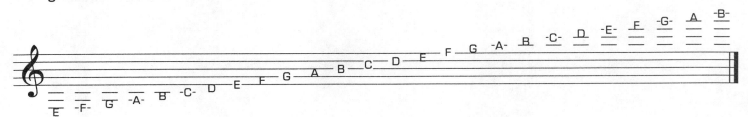

The staff is divided into **measures** by **bar lines**. A heavy double bar line marks the end of the music.

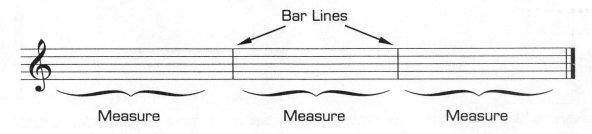

## Reading Tablature and Fretboard Diagrams

Tablature illustrates the location of notes on the neck of the guitar. This illustration compares the six strings of a guitar to the six lines of tablature.

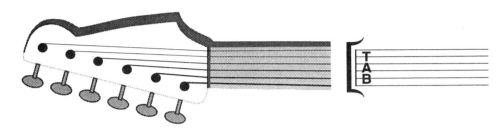

Notes are indicated by placing fret numbers on the strings. An "O" indicates an open string.

This tablature indicates to play the open, 1st and 3rd frets on the 1st string.

Tablature is usually used in conjunction with standard music notation. The rhythms and note names are indicated by the standard notation and the location of those notes on the guitar neck is indicated by the tablature.

Chords are often indicated in **chord block diagrams**. The vertical lines represent the strings and the horizontal line represent the frets. Scales are often indicated with guitar **fretboard diagrams**. Here the strings are horizontal and the frets are vertical.

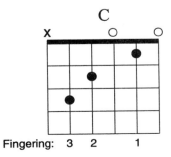

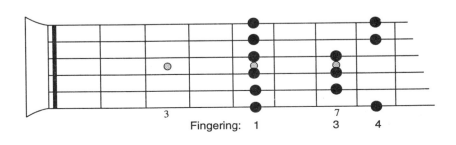

# Section Two: Open Position Chords

## The Six Basic Open Position Chords

These are the most fundamental chords to all styles of guitar playing. "Open" position chords contain open strings which ring out loud and clear. The sound of a ringing open chord is probably the most identifiable guitar sound there is. Whether you play acoustic or electric guitar, these six chords will be some of the main chords you will use throughout your lifetime.

**CD (5) The E Major Chord**

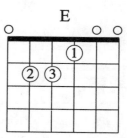

The dots indicate which notes to play with your finger, the open circles indicate open strings and "x" indicates a string that should not be played. The numbers under the chord frame indicate which left-hand finger to use. Play the E chord. Make sure you get a clear sound without any buzzing or muffled notes. Your fingertips should be placed just behind the fret—not on top of it or too far behind it. Also, the fingertips should be perpendicular to the fingerboard; if they lean at an angle they will interfere with the other strings and prevent them from ringing.

**CD (6) The A Major Chord**

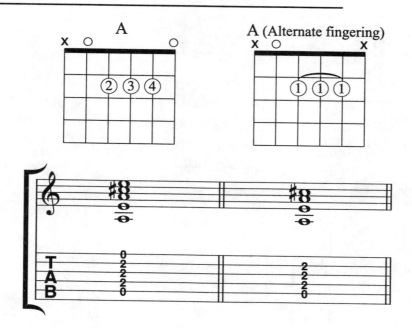

Notice that in the alternate fingering there is no 1st string E. This is OK, it's still an A chord.

**CD**
**(7) The D Major Chord**

The D chord uses just the top four strings. Play the chord making sure you can get a good clear, ringing tone.

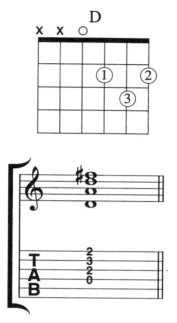

**Strumming:**

Relax your left-hand and strum with a constant down-up motion from your wrist. Strike the strings evenly with both the down-strum and, as your hand returns to playing position, with the up-strum.

Listen to the recording and when you're ready, play along.

**CD**
**(8) *Example 1: First Strumming Pattern***

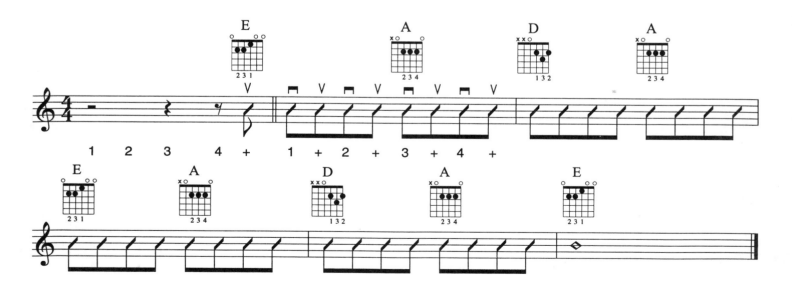

Note: Down-strums are indicated with this symbol: ⊓.  Up-strums are indicated with this symbol:

## G Major

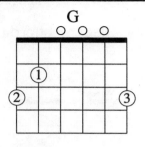

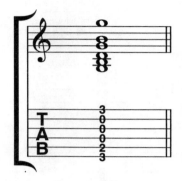

Tip: In order to play this chord cleanly, it is essential that you play on your fingertips, holding your fingers perpendicular to the neck. Keeping your left-hand thumb down in the center of the neck will help keep your fingers in the best position to avoid interfering with the other strings.

**CD 10** *Example 2*

Now try combining the G chord with the D chord. Notice both chords use the same three fingers:

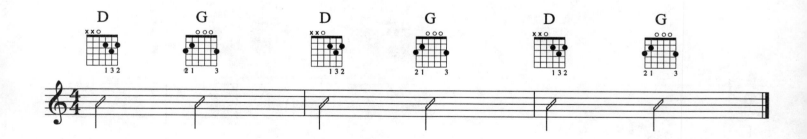

**CD 11 C Major**

Remember: Hold your fingers perpendicular to the neck making sure they touch only the strings they are playing and do not interfere with the other strings.

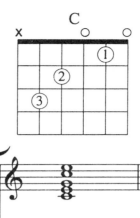

**CD 12** *Example 3*

Practice moving back and forth between the C and G chords.

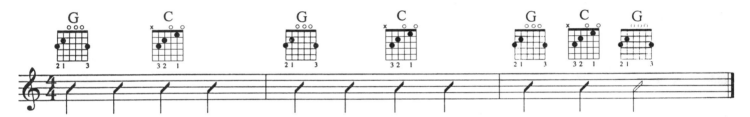

**CD 13 B7 Chord**

The G, D, C and E chords each contain three different notes. The B7 is a four-note chord (B, D♯, F♯, A).

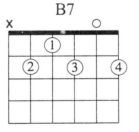

**CD 14** *Example 4*

Now try this next example which switches between the E and B7 chords.

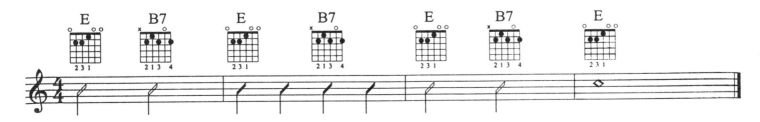

## The Blues Progression (in four keys)

The blues progression is the most common chord progression. The typical blues progression is 12 measures long and uses the 1st, 4th and 5th chords of the key. To find the 1st, 4th and 5th chords (usually indicated with Roman numerals: I, IV and V) simply count up through the alphabet from the key note.

For Example:

| Blues in the key of "A": | A | B | C | D | E | F | G | A |
|---|---|---|---|---|---|---|---|---|
| | I | | | IV | V | | | |

| Blues in the key of "G": | G | A | B | C | D | E | F | G |
|---|---|---|---|---|---|---|---|---|
| | I | | | IV | V | | | |

| Blues in the key of "E": | E | F | G | A | B | C | D | E |
|---|---|---|---|---|---|---|---|---|
| | I | | | IV | V | | | |

| Blues in the key of "D": | D | E | F | G | A | B | C | D |
|---|---|---|---|---|---|---|---|---|
| | I | | | IV | V | | | |

## Example 5: Strum Pattern A

The next progression can be played with a variety of "strum" patterns. First try this simple "quarter-note" (one strum per beat) pattern. It can be played with either your pick, for a clear, bright sound; or your thumb, which gives it a darker, warmer sound. Listen to the recording to hear the difference.

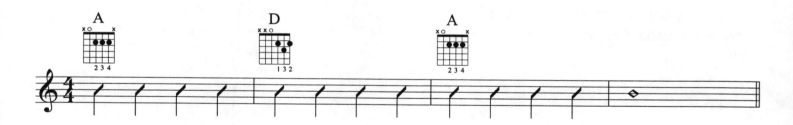

## Example 6: Strum Pattern B

This next pattern uses both down- and up-strokes of the pick. Your right hand should maintain a constant down-up motion, but you'll hit the strings on both the down-stroke, and on some of the up-strokes.

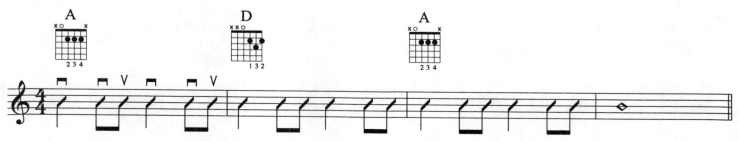

CD (16) **Example 7**

This strumming example takes the blues progression through four keys: A, G, E, and D. It uses just the six chords you've learned so far: A, D, E, G, C and B7. Play along with the recording using the two rhythms you've just learned. When you're comfortable with the chord changes, try making up some rhythms of your own.

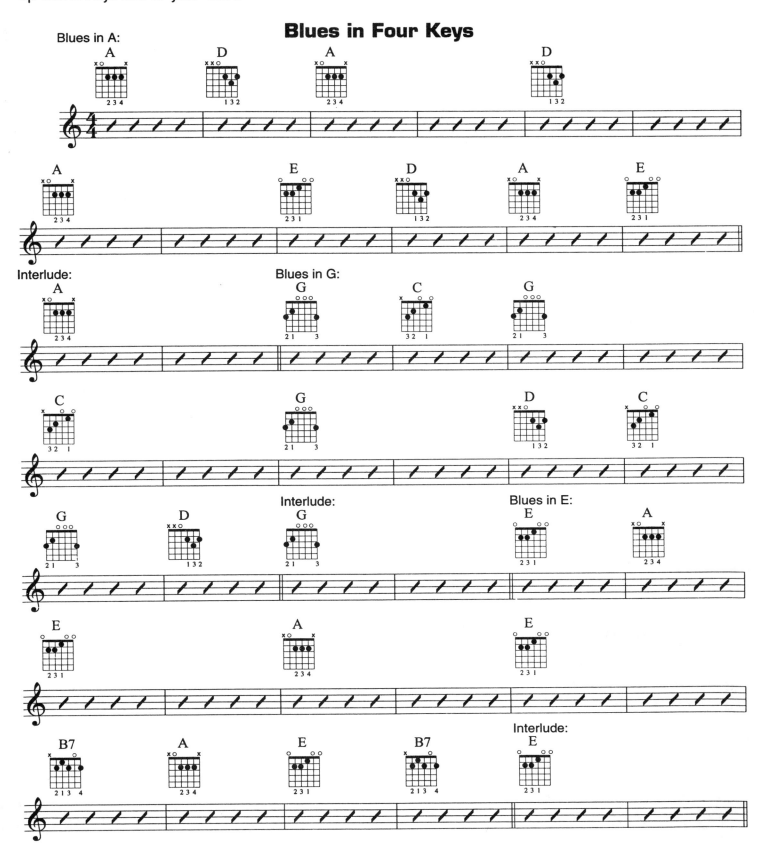

# Blues in Four Keys

**Blues in D:**

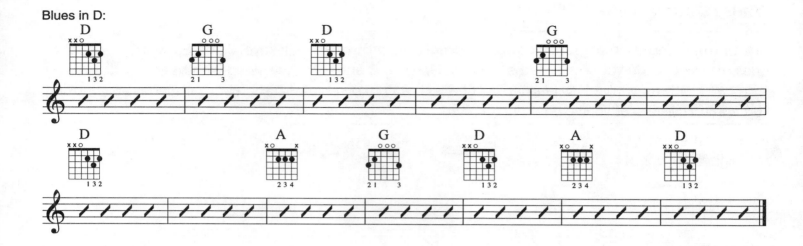

## Down-Up Strumming

As you've already seen in Example 6, picking (or strumming) consists of two elements: the down-stroke and the up-stroke. Again, your right hand should maintain a constant down-up motion, striking the strings on not only the down-stroke, but also on some of the up-strokes.

**CD (17) Example 8**

Here is a typical alternating strum pattern played over an E chord.

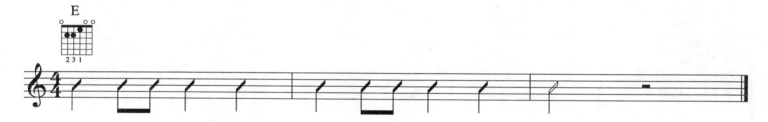

**CD (18) Example 9**

Now let's apply the strum pattern from the previous example to the chord progression: E - D - A - E.

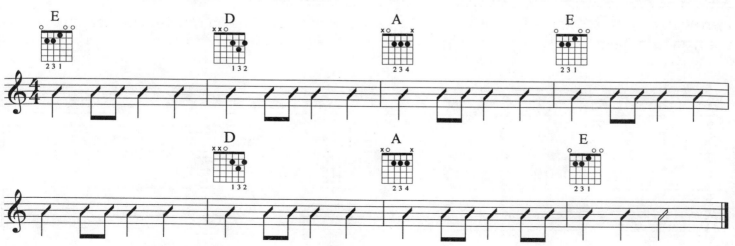

## Bass/Chord Strum Patterns

One of the most common acoustic guitar strumming techniques is the bass/chord strumming pattern. First play the bass note (the root) of the chord, then strum the rest of the chord.

**CD (19)** *Example 10*

Here is an example using an E chord. Play the lowest note (E on the 6th string) and then strum the higher strings. Use all down strokes.

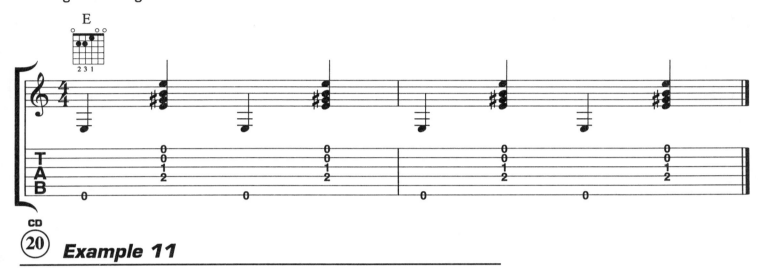

**CD (20)** *Example 11*

Here is an example using an A chord. Play the lowest note (A on the 5th string) and then strum the higher strings. It's okay to look down at your picking hand if that helps.

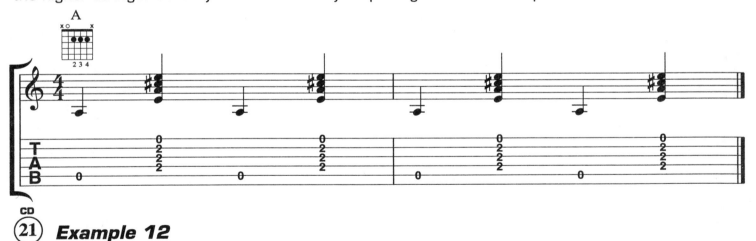

**CD (21)** *Example 12*

Here is an example using a D chord. Play the lowest note (D on the 4th string) and then strum the higher strings.

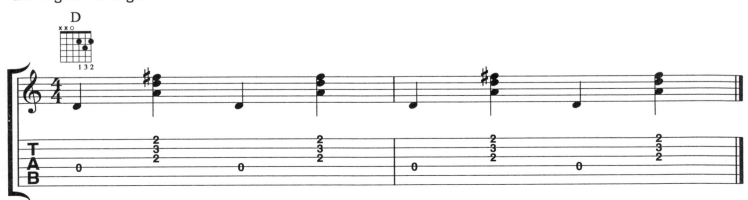

**CD**
**(22) Example 13**

Now try the bass/strum technique with the G chord. Again, play the lowest note (G on the 6th string) and then strum the higher strings.

**CD**
**(23) Example 14**

Now try the bass/strum technique on the C chord. The root is the 5th string "C."

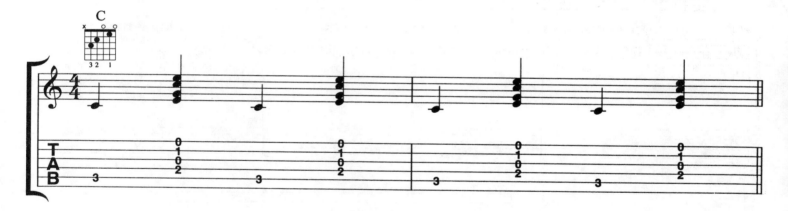

**CD**
**(24) Example 15**

Finally, let's try the bass/strum technique on the B7 chord. The root is the 5th string "B."

*Example 16*

Now put the bass/strum pattern in the context of a song using the chords G, C and D. Practice the example until you can shift smoothly from one chord to the next without stopping or breaking up the rhythm.

## The Alternating Bass/Strum Pattern

The most common variation on the bass/strum pattern is to alternate between two different bass notes.

**CD**
**(26)** *Example 17*

The simplest alternating bass pattern is to first play the lowest note, strum, then play the next highest bass note, then strum again. So for an E chord the pattern would be: 6th string E–strum– 5th string B–strum. Again, use all down-strokes.

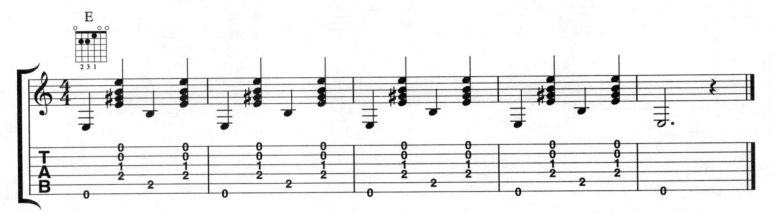

Note: Usually when playing alternating bass/chord patterns it sounds best to "skip" or "miss" the bass notes when you strum the chord.

**CD**
**(27)** *Example 18*     **Ex. 18A**

Now try the pattern over the A chord. Example 18A shows the previous pattern applied to the A chord. First play the 5th string A, strum, then play the 4th string E, then strum again.

**Ex. 18B**

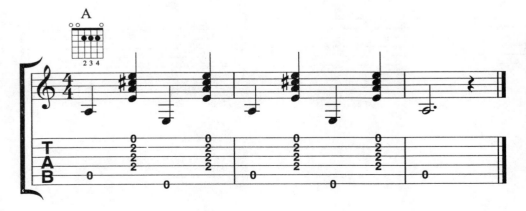

Example 18B shows a variation on the pattern: First play the 5th string A, strum, now instead of playing the 4th string E play the low 6th string E, then strum again. Again, use all down-strokes.

**CD**
**(28)** *Example 19*

**Ex. 19A**

Now try the pattern over the D chord. Example 19A shows the basic pattern applied to the D chord. First play the 4th string D, strum, then play the 3rd string A, then strum again.

Since the 3rd string A is a little too high to provide a good bass, try using the 5th string as the alternate bass note instead: First play the 4th string D, strum, now instead of playing the 3rd string A play the low 5th string A, then strum again.

**Ex. 19B**

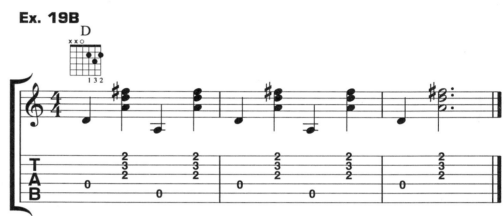

**CD**
**(29)** *Example 20*

**Ex. 20A**

Now try the pattern over the G chord. Example 20A alternates between the 6th string G and the 5th string B.

Example 20B alternates between the 6th string G and the 4th string D. (Again, notice how we "skip" the bass note "D" on the strum.)

**Ex. 20B**

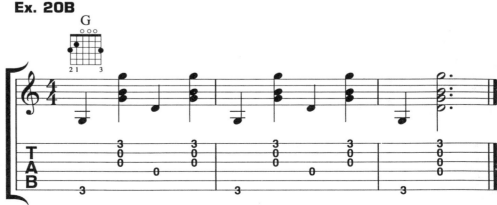

CD
(30) *Example 21*

For the C chord alternate between the 5th string C and the 4th string E.

**Ex. 21A**

Example 21B shows a nice variation on the alternating bass pattern. Play the 5th string C, strum, then shift your 3rd finger from the C to the 6th string G, then strum again. Notice that we only strum the top four strings. This pattern will take a little practice but soon you'll have it down.

**Ex. 21B**

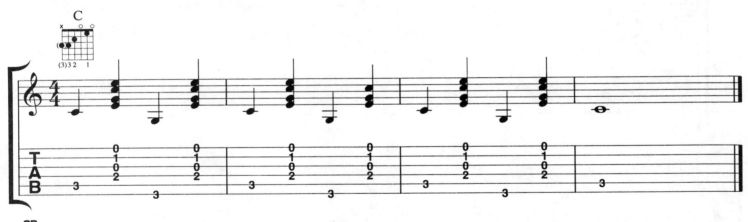

CD
(31) *Example 22*

We can apply the same type of patterns to the B7 chord. First try alternating between the 5th string B and the 4th string D♯.

**Ex. 22A**

Example 22B uses the same type of finger shifting as you used with the C chord in Example 21B. Play the 5th string B, strum, then shift your 2nd finger from the B to the 6th string F♯, then strum again.

**Ex. 22B**

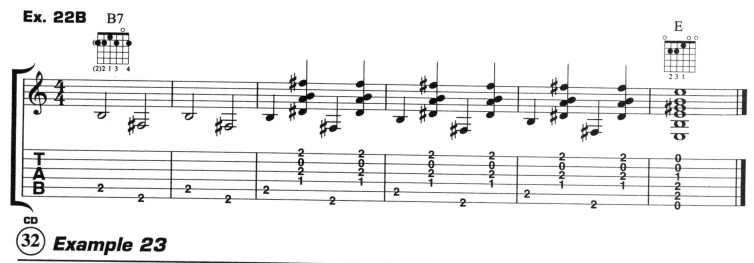

**CD**
**(32)** *Example 23*

This example combines all the chords you've learned with the alternating bass pattern.

CD
**(33)** *Chord Categories*

There are three categories of chords: Major, Minor and Dominant 7th. With these three types of chords you can play basically any pop or rock song. You already know five basic open position major chords: E, D, C, A and G.

**Minor Chords:** Minor chords differ from major chords by only one note: the 3rd. (To find the "3rd" count up three from the root (1). By lowering the 3rd of any major chord one fret it becomes a minor chord.

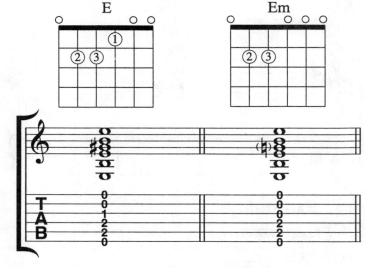

CD
**(34)** *Example 24*

Play back and forth between the E and Em chords:

Notice again that the difference between the A and Am, and D and Dm chords is only one note (the 3rd).

CD
**(35)**

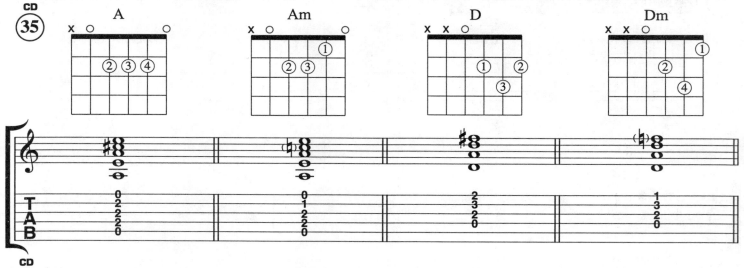

CD
**(36)** *Example 25*

Play back and forth between the A and Am chords:

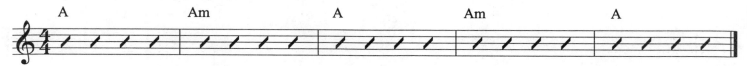

CD
**(37)** *Example 26*

Play back and forth between the D and Dm chords:

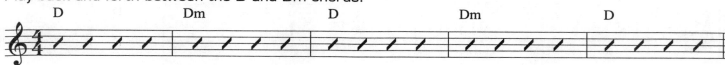

**CD**
**(38)** **Dominant Chords:** Dominant chords differ from major chords by the addition of one note: the 7th. (To find the "7th" count up seven from the root (1)). Adding the 7th to a major chord makes it a dominant 7th chord.

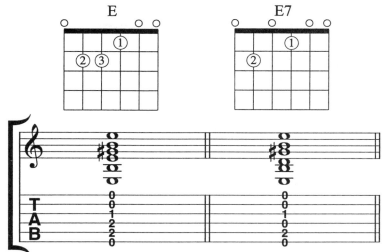

**CD**
**(39)** *Example 27*

Play back and forth between the E and E7 chords. Listen closely to the difference in sound the one new note makes:

**CD**
**(40)** The difference between the A and A7, and D and D7 chords is again the addition of one note: the 7th.

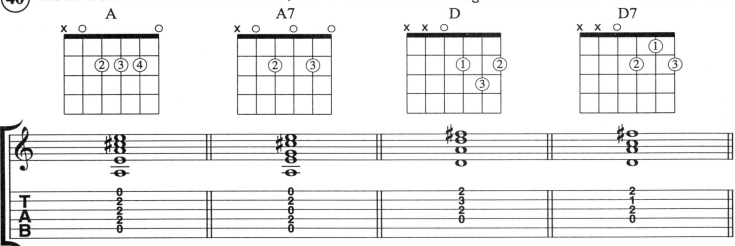

**CD**
**(41)** *Example 28*

Play back and forth between the A and A7 chords:

**CD**
**(42)** *Example 29*

Play back and forth between the D and D7 chords:

**CD**
**43** The open position G chord can be converted to a dominant chord as shown here. Try fingering the G chord with your 2nd, 3rd and 4th fingers. This will make the change to G7 easier.

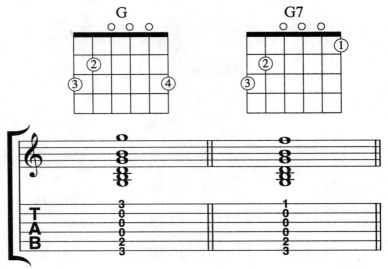

**CD**
**44** *Example 30*

Play back and forth between the G and G7 chords:

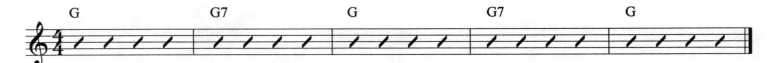

**CD**
**45** Now try converting the C to a C7. This is done by adding the 4th finger to the 3rd string.

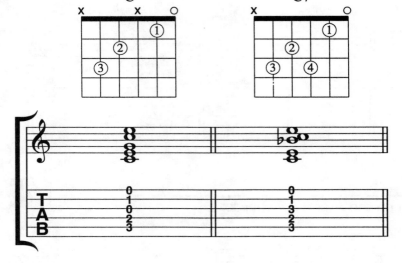

**CD**
**46** *Example 31*

Play back and forth between the C and C7 chords:

# Section Three: Fingerpicking

So far, all the music in this book has been playable with either a pick or your thumb. Fingerpicking involves using the thumb and fingers independently of one another. This gives you the ability to play separate bass lines and melodies, all at the same time.

 **Example 32**

Hold an E chord. With your thumb play an alternating bass from the 6th string E to the 4th string E. Gently rest your index finger on the high E string while playing the steady quarter-note alternating bass with your thumb.

## Example 33

Continue to hold the E chord while playing the alternating bass with your thumb. Play the high E string with an upstroke of your index finger. The up-stroke of your index finer should happen at the same time as the down-stroke of your thumb. Notice that the bass notes (thumb) are written stems down and the melody notes (index finger) are written stems up.

 **Example 34**

Now trying plucking the high E string with your index finger in-between the thumb strokes. This is a little tricky at first. Keep playing this example until it feels easy and natural.

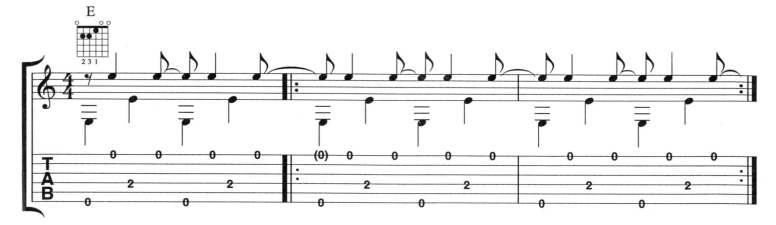

**CD**
**(49)** *Example 35*

The real beauty of this technique becomes apparent when you begin developing patterns that mix plucking on the beat (with the bass note) and plucking off the beat (in-between the bass notes). Practice this example until the alternating thumb becomes automatic—as if it is functioning independently of your fingers.

**CD**
**(50)** *Example 36*

Now try applying the same pattern to an A chord. Begin with just the alternating thumb, then add the index finger on the beat, then with the index finger in-between the beats and then the complete pattern as in the previous example.

**CD**
**(51)** *Example 37*

Now apply the fingerpicking pattern to a G chord. As you begin to feel comfortable with these fingerpicking patterns, it would be a good idea to begin substituting your right-hand middle finger and then your ring finger for your index finger on the top string. Eventually you will want to use all three fingers in varying combinations.

**CD**
**(52)** *Example 38*

In Example 19 we began using an alternate bass note for the D chord: the 5th string A below the 4th
string D. In this fingerpicking example your thumb will alternate between the 4th string D and both the
3rd and 5th string A notes. Practice just the thumb movement until it feels natural (Example 38A).
Then add your index finger (Example 38B).

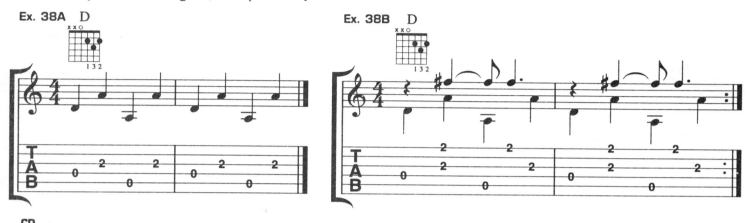

**CD**
**(53)** *Example 39*

For the C chord your thumb will alternate between the 5th string C, the 4th string E and the 6th string
G. As in Example 21B you will have to shift your 3rd finger back and forth from C to G. Practice just the
thumb movement until it feels natural (Example 39A). Then add your index finger (Example 39B).

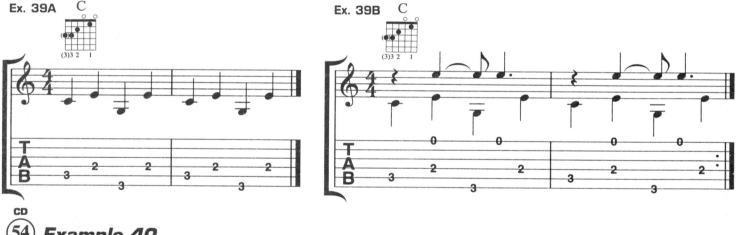

**CD**
**(54)** *Example 40*

Now apply the previous pattern to the B7 chord. You will have to shift your 2nd finger back and forth
from the 5th to the 6th strings (see Example 22B). Again, practice just the thumb movement until it
feels natural (Example 40A). Then add your index finger (Example 40B).

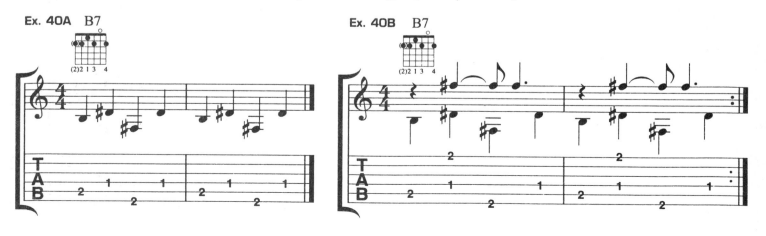

**CD 55** *Example 41*

This example combines the fingerpicking patterns with a complete chord progression.

Once the alternating thumb begins to feel "automatic" you'll be able to begin developing many variations on this pattern. Experiment with adding your middle and ring fingers in developing new patterns.

# Section Four: Hammer-Ons and Pull-Offs with Chords

One way to add new sounds and make your chords more interesting is to add and subtract certain notes from the chords as you play. We will use two different slurring techniques to add and subtract these notes:

1) A **hammer-on** is when you push (or "hammer") a left-hand finger onto a string with enough force to sound the note without using your picking hand.

2) A **pull-off** is when you release a left-hand finger from the string with a slight downward motion—actually plucking the string with the tip of your left-hand finger; again, sounding the note without using your picking hand.

## *Example 42*

We can add a note to the E chord by "hammering" the 4th finger down on the 3rd string. This changes the chord from an E major to an E suspended.

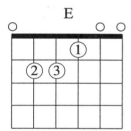  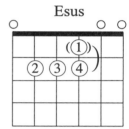

Play along with the recording. Then try making up some of your own patterns, switching between the E and Esus chords.

## *Example 43*

We can add other notes to the E chord. These diagrams indicate an added note on the 2nd string. This changes the chord from an E major to an E6. The next two diagrams show an added note on the 1st string. This alters the chord from an E major to an Eadd9. The notes are "added" using the hammer-on technique, and released using the pull-off technique.

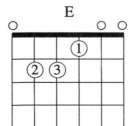  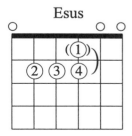  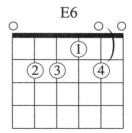  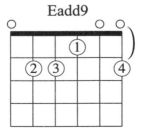

Again, play along with the recording. Then try making up some of your own patterns switching between the E/E6 and E/Eadd9 chords.

**CD**
**(58) Example 44**

By moving your 4th finger up one fret you can add a "D" note to the A chord forming a Dsus. By lifting your 4th finger off the 2nd string you form an Asus2 chord

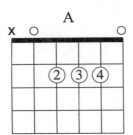
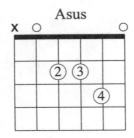
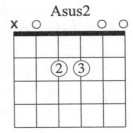

Again, play along with the recording. Then try making up some of your own patterns, switching between the A, Asus and Asus2 chords.

**CD**
**(59) Example 45**

By "hammering" your 4th finger on the 1st string G you can change the D chord to Dsus and by "pulling-off" your 2nd finger you can form Dsus2.

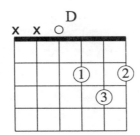
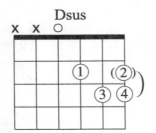
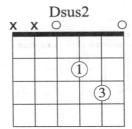

Again, play along with the recording. Then try making up some of your own patterns switching between the D, Dsus and Dsus2.

**CD**
**(60) Example 46**

If you finger the G chord with your 2nd, 3rd and 4th fingers your 1st finger will then be available for use on the 2nd string to form the Gsus chord.

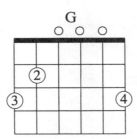
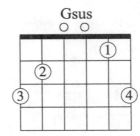

*Example 47*

For the C chord, the 4th finger can be hammered on to the 4th string to form a Csus chord. The 3rd finger can be pulled-off the 4th string to form a Csus2.

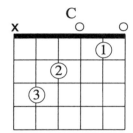
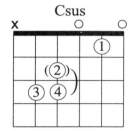
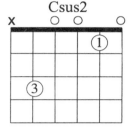

*Example 48*

Minor chords can be embellished in the same way as major chords—by adding and subtracting notes, usually using the hammer-on and pull-off slurring techniques.

For A minor, adding the 4th finger on the 2nd string changes A minor to Asus. Pulling-off the 1st finger forms an Asus2.

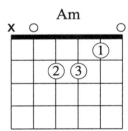
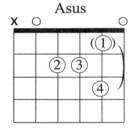

For D minor, adding the 4th finger on the 1st string changes D minor to Dsus. Pulling-off the 1st finger forms a Dsus2.

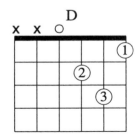
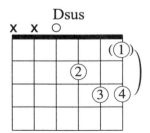
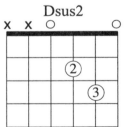

Again, play along with the recording. Then try making up some of your own patterns, switching between the various chords and their "colorations."

## The Capo

So far, all of the chords you've learned have been first position "open" string chord voicings. Using just these chords you are well on your way towards playing many popular songs in the keys of C, G, D, A and E.

**Example 49**

With a capo you can transpose these chord fingerings to work in almost any key. For example, if you place the capo at the 3rd fret, all of the open string notes will be transposed up three frets. So if you then finger an E chord it will sound as a G chord, an A chord will sound as a C chord, etc.

G (E fingering)
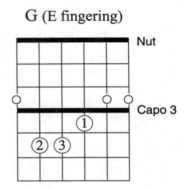

C (A fingering)
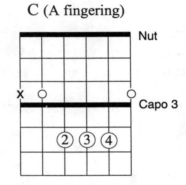

F (D fingering)
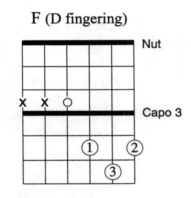

B♭ (G fingering)
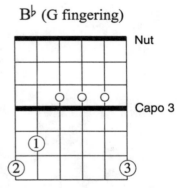

E♭ (C fingering)
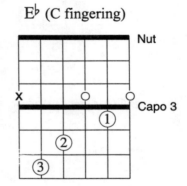

D7 (B7 fingering)
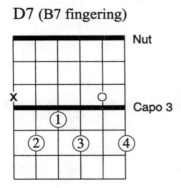

The capo is especially handy when you want to accompany a singer (or yourself). When the key of a song is too low, you can always bring it up higher by using the capo.

It is usually best to think of the song in the "fingering" key, locating the capo at whichever fret places the chords at a good pitch for the singer.

# Section Five: Barre Chords

There are two types of barre chords: those with their root on the 6th string and those with their root on the 5th string. Before we learn the barre chords lets first learn the notes on those two strings.

**CD**
**(64) *Example 50***

This diagram shows the location of the natural (no sharps or flats) notes on the 6th string. It is useful to remember that there is a whole step (two frets) between all adjacent natural notes except for "E - F" and "B - C" which are separated by a half-step (one fret).

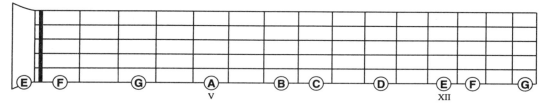

Here are the notes and tablature for the notes on the "E" string. Play these notes until they are memorized.

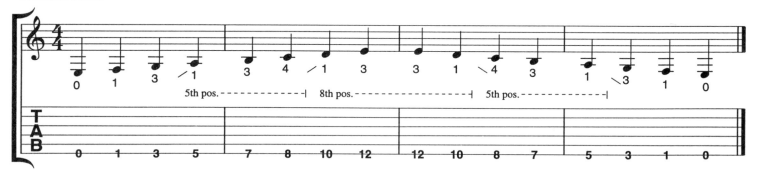

**CD**
**(65) *Example 51***

This diagram shows the location of the natural (no sharps or flats) notes on the 5th string. Again, remember that there is a whole-step (two frets) between all adjacent natural notes except for "E - F" and "B - C" which are separated by a half-step (one fret).

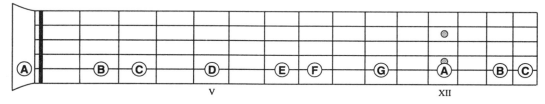

Here are the notes and tablature for the notes on the "A" string. Play these notes until they are memorized.

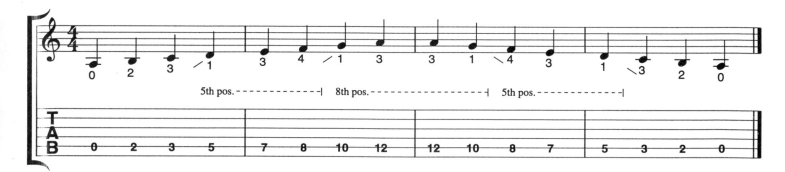

## The "E" Type Barre Chord

So far we've only worked on open position chords. With barre chords you can leave the open position and play all around the neck.

**Barre Chords:** A barre chord is a chord in which two or more of the strings are played by one finger laying across those strings forming a "barre."

### (66) Example 52

The most popular type of barre chord is based on the common E chord. To form the barre chord:

  1) Re-finger the E chord with your 2nd, 3rd and 4th fingers.

  2) Shift your fingers up one fret.

  3) Lay your 1st finger across all six strings at the 1st fret.

Practice each of the following chords, then try moving the barre chord to each fret on the neck and saying the name of the chord aloud.

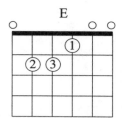
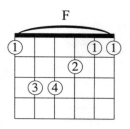
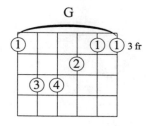
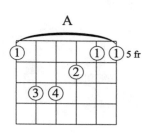

Tip: To add strength to your index finger barre, turn that finger slightly to the side so that the hard outside edge of the finger forms the barre; not the soft, fleshy part on the inside.

### (67) Example 53

Now convert the E minor to a barre chord. Again, practice each of these chords and then try playing them all over the neck, saying the name of the chord aloud.

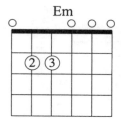
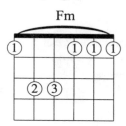
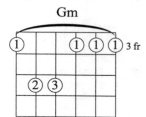
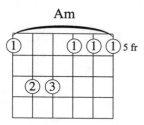

## Example 54

Now convert the E7 to a barre chord. Again, practice each of these chords and then try playing them all over the neck, saying the name of the chord aloud.

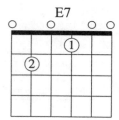
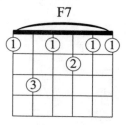
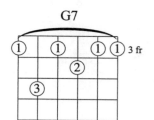
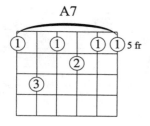

## The "A" Type Barre Chord

The next most popular type of barre chord is based on the common A chord. To form the "A" type barre chord:

1) Shift your 2nd, 3rd and 4th fingers up one fret.

2) Lay your 1st finger across the top five strings at the 1st fret.

 *Example 55*

Practice each of the following chords, then try moving the barre chord to each fret and saying the name of the chord aloud. Notice the optional fingering which requires a 3rd finger barre across the middle strings. When using this optional fingering you'll probably mute the 1st string with your 3rd finger. Practice both fingerings and see which works best for you.

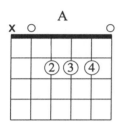 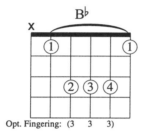 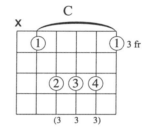 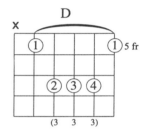

 *Example 56*

Now convert the A minor to a barre chord. Again, practice each of these chords and then try playing them all over the neck, saying the name of the chord aloud.

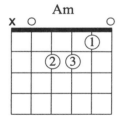 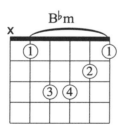 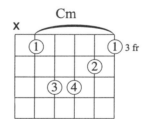 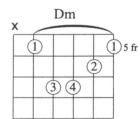

## Example 57

Now convert the A7 to a barre chord. Again, practice each of these chords and then try playing them all over the neck, saying the name of the chord aloud.

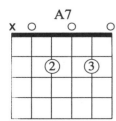 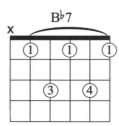 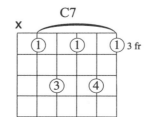 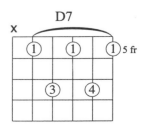

## Guitar Chord Chart

---

# OPEN POSITION CHORDS

**A**
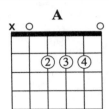

**Am**
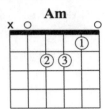

**A7**

**B7**
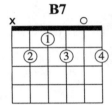

**C**
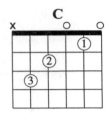

**C7**
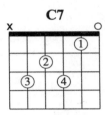

**D**
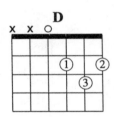

**Dm**
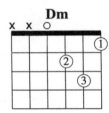

**D7**
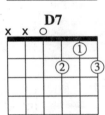

**E**
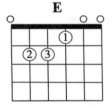

**Em**
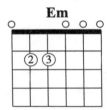

**E7**
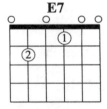

**F**
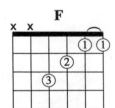

**G**
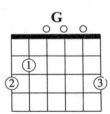

**G7**
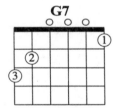

# BARRE CHORDS

**"E type" Barre**
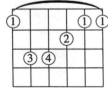

**"Em type" Barre**
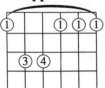

**"E7 type" Barre**
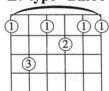

**"A type" Barre**
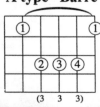

**"Am type" Barre**

**"A7 type" Barre**
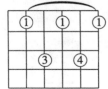